HOPE IN THE WILDERNESS

BY
PATRICIA MORGAN

ACKNOWLEDGMENT

Writing this book has me reflecting on my social worker when I was nine years old. I said I wanted to be like Ms. Lewis when I grew up.

Ms. Lewis, I am like you, with a career in social work so thanks for being my mentor at a young age. To, My Professor at Marygrove College for encouraging me to write my story.

Well, Professor, I finally wrote my book after pondering why should I because so many people have experienced foster care, molestation, homelessness, mental health issues, etc. But guess what they did not experience my experience of being a foster child, being adopted, wanting to know and be accepted by my biological family, my fears and tears, shame, longing to know both my biological father and brother and losing a career job due to discrimination.

On another note, In the King James Version of the Bible, the phrase "when I was hungry" appears in Matthew 25:35-40:

"For I was an hungred, and ye gave me meat: I was thirsty, and ye gave me drink: I was a stranger, and ye took me in: naked, and ye clothed me: I was sick, and ye visited me: I was in prison, and ye came unto me.

As a result, of God's earthly helping hands I would be remiss not to acknowledge all (and you know who you are) who were there for me in my emotional downcast darkest

i

hour as they fulfilled the scripture and fed me when I was hungry, gave me drink and took me in. Additionally, I must acknowledge and thank my Pastor wife for her counsel, firm but nurturing redirecting, monetary and other gifting and most of all her compassion and concern when I lost my job and became homeless, she did not turn a deaf hear or blinded eyes. Again, thank you to her all of God's helping hands.

The irony of these life experiences, challenges, and barriers will show that even in the state of despair and hardship it will eventually prepare me for my current social work career to help others who are oppressed, homeless, and experiencing social injustice. Like Romans 8: 28 states, and we know that all things work together for good to them that love God, to them who are the called according to his purpose.

Further, I am grateful to the editors and my Project manager who was very patient, inspiring me telling me God chose me to share my story.

DEDICATION

Lord I just want to take this time to say thank you for choosing me for such a time as this heeding to your plan Jeremiah 29:11 "For I know the plans I have for you declares the Lord.

Plans to prosper you and not to harm you, plans to give you a hope and a future." I did not understand everything I went through while I was going through the adversities but one thing, I can say with assurance is that trusting you has increased my faith as I rely on your word and your plan to give me hope in the wilderness

FOREWORD

Life takes us down paths we don't always understand. *Having Hope in the Wilderness* is my story of resilience, faith, and overcoming challenges. It is the journey of a little girl, placed in foster care, longing for love and connection, who grew into a woman determined to find purpose through every obstacle she faced.

From my earliest days in foster homes, longing to be loved, to losing my job and finding myself homeless, this journey has been anything but easy. Yet, through every hardship, I found strength I didn't know I had and faith that carried me when nothing else could. This story is my way of sharing that even in the darkest times, there is hope to be found.

The decision to write this book came after much thought and encouragement. I wondered if my story was worth telling—after all, many people face challenges. But then I realized that no one else has lived my life. No one else has felt my pain, my determination, or my moments of triumph in the same way.

This book is a testament to the power of faith and perseverance. It is written for anyone who feels lost or uncertain, for those who need to know that better days are ahead. It is my way of giving back, of saying, "You are not alone."

Thank you to everyone who encouraged me to tell my story and who stood by me through my darkest moments. I hope this book inspires you to keep moving forward, no matter what wilderness you are facing.

Patricia Morgan

ABOUT THE AUTHOR

Born Patricia Alexander in Detroit, Michigan, at Herman Keifer Hospital to an unwed mother and raised in six foster homes, Patricia was finally adopted by the seventh foster family. Patricia shares that while in foster homes experiences an abundance of emotions like fear, sadness, low self-esteem, anger, bitterness, and abandonment. confusion and desire to belong and be loved by family. Patricia often wondered why her mother did not want her and even more why her biological family did not want her, but her biological brother was raised by her maternal grandmother.

Patricia was finally adopted but that did not come without challenges like having her name changed, getting pregnant one month before graduating high school, and marrying her son's father. The marriage lasted four years and then Patricia experienced juggling part-time jobs, relied on aid for dependent children, and dipped in and out of school. I did get my Associate degree as a Social Work Technician at Jordon College before finally getting a job with the United States Postal Service for about ten years before getting removed due to unfair practices.

After losing a Postal job Patricia became homeless and history repeated itself. Patricia lived in seven homes from her church community living with seven different families. I worked part-time as a receptionist at a Beauty Shop enduring emotional abuse before going to Marygrove College, getting my bachelor's of social work degree, and then to Wayne

State University obtaining my Master of Social Work degree.

Finally, after graduating getting a job at Team Mental Health on 3rd November 2014, where my career allowed me to work in different disciplines as a Care Coordinator, Clinical Therapist, Intake Specialist, Support Coordinator and more importantly still working at Passing my LMSW clinical exam. In school, they ask the cohorts why they choose social work. My reply was, "I did not choose it. Social work chose me from a little girl wanting to be like Ms. Lewis."

Table of Contents

Acknowledgment I

Dedication III

About The Author V

Chapter 1. Early Life In Foster Care 1

Chapter 2. School Days And Social Challenges 6

Chapter 3. Life Challenges 9

Chapter 4. Losing And Rebuilding Life 16

Chapter 5. Turning Struggles Into Strengths 22

Chapter 6. From Homelessness To Hope 29

Chapter 7. Piecing Together The Past 34

Chapter 8. Through The Storm, We Stand 38

Chapter 9. Shaped By Shadows, Guided By Light 42

CHAPTER 1.
EARLY LIFE IN FOSTER CARE

"Sometimes the strength of motherhood is greater than natural laws." — Barbara Kingsolver

I came into this world on Christmas Day in 1959, in the busy halls of Herman Keifer Hospital. As a new, nine-pound baby girl, I spent my first three months there before moving into the foster care system. The reason, I was told, was that my mother suffered from schizophrenia. As a child, this term was just a vague, scary word that didn't fully explain why she couldn't be with me. I often felt it was just an excuse for not wanting me.

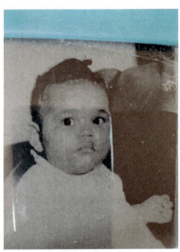

As years passed, my career led me to learn more about mental health, and with it, a deeper understanding of schizophrenia. This complex condition can deeply affect a person's ability to care for others, altering their perception of reality and making everyday tasks daunting. It can turn the world into a frightening place, where loved ones might seem like strangers.

Through my work, I met many brave individuals battling similar issues, and I saw up close the challenges and the triumphs in their lives. These experiences helped me piece together a clearer image of my mother's struggles. I realized that her decision to place me in foster care wasn't an act of abandonment but of immense bravery and love. She chose a safer life for me, one that she alone could not provide at that time.

This insight changed everything. I began to see her choice not as a loss but as a sacrifice made for my well-being. It brought me to a place of forgiveness and deep appreciation for her courage. It was a silent act of love, ensuring I had a chance at a better life, even if it meant she couldn't be a part of it.

My memories of my first foster home are blurry, shrouded in the fog of early childhood and the brief time I spent there.

The second home was a stark contrast. It was run by an elderly couple steeped in traditional values. "You will address us as Father and Mother," the stern voice of my foster father echoed in the dining room on my first evening there. His words were firm, setting the tone for my new life under their roof. They instilled in me the importance of manners—"Yes, sir," "Yes, ma'am," "No, thank you," "Yes, please"—values that I carry with gratitude today.

Church was non-negotiable. Every Sunday, alongside my foster siblings, I was dressed in my best, our shoes polished to a shine. "Children, remember your verses," my foster mother would remind us as we filed into the car. I learned prayers and scriptures, my young mind weaving through the verses of the Bible.

Despite these structured, disciplined days, my life in that home wasn't devoid of warmth. I recall a particular Christmas when my foster parents gifted me Fisher Price toys—vivid flashes of joy that I still remember distinctly even at sixty-four.

Yet, not all my foster homes provided such security. One memory, darker and more searing than the rest, clings to me with chilling clarity. It was in a car, parked outside a supermarket. My foster mother was inside, and I was alone with him—my foster father. His voice was a whisper, laced with menace, "You are not to tell anyone," he said, as his hands betrayed the trust every child should have in a parent.

I did eventually speak up. First to my foster mother, who dismissed my words, protecting her husband over protecting me? My determination didn't end there. I turned to my social worker, who took immediate action, though my foster mother maintained her husband's innocence.

Reflecting on these memories at sixty-four, I can see the lifelong impact they have had. It's disheartening when I hear, "You just need to get over that and move on." Such statements trivialize the profound and lasting effects of abuse. Through my career in social work, I've learned that all behavior has a cause, and it's crucial to listen carefully to what children are trying to express, often without words.

Talking to people, I sometimes encounter those who use religion to dismiss the real pain of such experiences. "You just have to forgive and let that go," they advise. While forgiveness is a powerful step, true healing requires understanding, support, and accountability. Holding the perpetrator accountable is as important as supporting the victim through their healing journey.

However, there were moments in my childhood that shone brightly against the tougher times. I remember how it felt when the social worker would pick me up from school for appointments or visits to my biological mom. My classmates would throw curious looks my way, whispering and wondering. It was embarrassing, sure, but it also made me feel a bit like a mystery, which wasn't all bad.

One of my favorite places during those visits was the big, peaceful dollhouse at the Children's Aid Society. I could lose myself in that little world, forgetting the complexities of my own life for a while. During those moments, playing quietly, I'd watch my biological mother from the corner of my eye, always pondering why I seemed to have so many mothers yet never daring to ask.

As I got older, I understood more about my situation, but back then, it was just another part of my life. Another bright spot was learning my first Christmas speech for church when I was about eight. Standing in front of the congregation, I recited, St Luke 2:11 "For unto you is bor this day in the city of David a Savior which is Christ the Lord." I felt a rush of pride with every word, feeling connected to something bigger than myself.

These experiences, as simple as they might seem, helped shape me. They taught me about resilience and finding light in the shadows. Life in foster care was a patchwork of homes and experiences—some good, some bad. Like the time one of my foster mothers cruelly joked about sending me away. She woke me in the middle of the night and told me to pack my clothes because I was moving to another home. Then, with a harsh laugh, she said it was all a joke. I went back to bed, but not to sleep. I lay there, a bundle of nerves, never sure when the ground would shift again.

That night left a mark, igniting a storm of anxiety that I wouldn't understand or name for many years. It was an early lesson in trust—or rather, the lack of it—which made me wary but also strangely strong. It taught me to mask my fears with a smile, a skill that became second nature long before masks became a part of everyday life during the pandemic. Through it all, I wore my own invisible mask, learning to hide my feelings from a world that often didn't seem to care.

CHAPTER 2.
SCHOOL DAYS AND SOCIAL CHALLENGES

"Identity is a robe you wear, a robe adorned by experiences and woven by your own choices." — Celeste Ng

At thirteen, I landed in what would be my last foster home—a place that would soon become my permanent family. But even in this fresh start, there was a catch: my new mom wanted to change my birth name. She believed strongly in the power of names. She was worried about how it would look to others to have two daughters with the same name.

This made me wonder sometimes. If my name was such an issue, maybe she shouldn't have brought me into her family. Reluctantly, I chose a new name, hoping it would help me blend in and feel accepted. But inside, it felt like I was losing a part of myself.

As time passed, this new name just didn't feel right. It was like wearing someone else's shoes—I could walk in them, but they never fit comfortably. I longed for the name my birth mother had given me, the one that truly belonged to me. Eventually, I found the courage to take action. I went to probate court to get my birth name back.

The courtroom was intimidating, its silence echoing with the weight of decisions that could change lives. When the judge, in his formal tone, asked if I wanted to keep 'LaTonya' as my middle name, emotions overwhelmed me. I felt a mix of fear and nerves, realizing the significance of what I was about to reclaim.

Choosing to restore my birth name was more than a legal formality—it was a reclaiming of my identity and a tribute to my roots. Each step towards the judge felt like a step back towards myself. With each word I spoke, I felt stronger, and more connected to my true self.

That day, I declared my choice loud and clear: I wanted my original name back. Each syllable of my name was a piece of my history, a mark of where I had come from. It was a powerful moment of taking control, not just of my name, but of my story.

This experience taught me the true value of being authentic. It showed me that the most important acceptance is accepting yourself. It was a lesson in integrity—standing up for who I am, not just who others want me to be.

I told the judge to keep 'LaTonya' as my middle name, hoping it would ease the conversation when I explained to my mother that I preferred to be called by my birth name, Patricia. For me, Patricia was more than just a name. It was who I was from birth until I entered a home where having the same name as the biological daughter overshadowed my feelings. It seemed my comfort was less important than what others might think of two sisters sharing a name.

Changing my name back wasn't just a personal decision; it meant updating everything—my birth certificate, school records, work documents, driver's license, and even my social security. I remember my employer announcing to all my coworkers that they should now address me as Patricia. Most adjusted well, but one coworker resisted, saying, "I can't get with that. I've been calling you LaTonya." Eventually, though, she came around to respecting my request.

Years later, one of my favorite classes at Wayne State University was on grief and loss. It was here that I learned grief encompasses more than mourning someone's death—it also includes the loss of one's identity. Identity shapes how we see ourselves and how others perceive us. According to a Psychology Today article from July 14, 2021, it's about our roles in social groups and the labels others might assign to us.

Even now, the grief and loss of my name linger. Some people, perhaps out of habit or disregard, still call me LaTonya. It's astounding how this aspect of my adoption—this enforced name change—continues to affect me during major life events and moments of emotional stress. This was highlighted when I received my associate's and bachelor's degrees, each bearing a different first name, a constant reminder of my fragmented identity.

As I go through the complexities of identity and acceptance, I realize more and more that being called Patricia is not just about preference. It's about asserting the person I've always been—right from the start...

CHAPTER 3.
LIFE CHALLENGES

After reclaiming my birth name, another life-changing event was just around the corner. The month before graduating high school, I discovered I was pregnant. The morning sickness was unbearable, and the thought of telling my mother filled me with dread. Day after day, I mentally rehearsed how to break the news to her, struggling to find the right words.

Eventually, I decided it wasn't just my burden to bear. I told my son's father that he needed to be the one to tell my mother with me. We were in this together, after all. That day, feeling overwhelmed, I leaned my head on the table, trying to steady myself. My mother's reaction was one of sadness and concern. "What are you going to do?" she asked. The silence that followed hung heavy in the air.

Soon after, I moved in with my sister-in-law-to-be. My son's father and I got married, but our marriage only lasted four years. After our divorce, I embarked on the journey of being a single mother. I juggled part-time jobs, relied on aid for dependent children, and dipped in and out of school. My personal life was a string of fleeting relationships that never seemed to last.

In 1988, a trip to Chicago with my biological mother and son brought unexpected emotional challenges. We stayed with my aunt, and one day, my great-aunt took me to a dark, unwelcoming institution to see another aunt. She kept repeating, "I want my mother." The visit overwhelmed me, and all I could do was cry and long to leave. My aunt was furious at my great-aunt for taking me there, saying it was too much for us to handle.

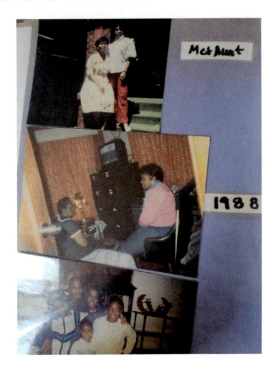

After taking back my birth name and handling the surprise of my pregnancy, I faced another tough moment. This time, I received a phone call from a staff at the Assisting Living Home where my mother resided stating, that she was taken to St John Hospital by ambulance for confrontation and biting a resident. It was during a visit to see my birth mother at the assisted living home where she now stayed. She was really upset, denying she had bitten another resident. "I did not bite that woman," she said loudly and angrily.

I had visited her many times before, at the Children's Aid Society and other homes, but I had never seen her like this. She seemed really confused and kept talking angrily about her past, blaming people who she said had hurt her. It was hard to know if what she was saying was all true because I wasn't there with her back then.

Seeing her this upset made me really sad. It showed me how deep her pain was and how much her past still bothered her. This visit made me understand even more why my job in mental health is so important. It reminded me to always be kind and patient with people, as you never fully know what they have gone through.

Each visit with my mother seemed to peel back another layer of the unknown, but one day something truly unexpected happened. While we were chatting, my mother suddenly looked scared and said quietly, "That man is trying to hurt me." She pointed towards the door with wide eyes. I quickly looked over, heart racing, but there was no one there. That's when it hit me—my mother was seeing things that weren't there.

On a different day, out of nowhere, she said to me, "Patricia, you can go to the house and take whatever you want." Her words were mysterious and left me more puzzled than ever. Why would she say that? What did she mean?

Then, a moment came that changed everything. On April 22, 2008, I sat with my mother singing two of my favorite songs, 'Amazing Grace' and 'Hold to God's Unchanging Hand.' My mother passed away. She found peace, leaving behind all her struggles. I remember calling my Pastor right after she died. He asked me gentle questions over the phone, "Were you with anyone? How did you get to the hospital?" It felt like he was trying to make sure I wasn't alone. I told him I had taken the bus by myself, feeling the loneliness sink in.

He also asked if I knew any of my biological family. "Yes, I know my aunt in Chicago," I told him. He suggested I call her to let the rest of the family know.

Meanwhile, my Pastor asked me to go to the desk and ask the staff to page a mutual clergy friend we both knew and ask her to call him. My Pastor was concerned about me taking the bus back home or the place where I was staying in my grief-stricken moment. The hospital staff summoned the clergy friend to my mother's room and when she entered, she gave her condolence prayed and told me my Pastor wanted her to take me home since he was unable to be present at this moment.

At my biological mother's funeral, my feelings were all mixed up. It was especially tough when my adopted mom walked me up to the casket for one last look. As we moved closer, I kept wondering what she might be thinking. Here she was, helping her daughter say goodbye to another mom. People often say you only have one mother, but that day, there were clearly two important mothers in my life.

The funeral had music and scriptures but the eulogy was different due to my Pastor not knowing my mother. The eulogy became more about me which brought lots of laughter, and the audience stood to their feet clapping as my Pastor described me in his comical way in place of not knowing my biological mother. Even in the midst of the laughter, for me, it felt like a storm of emotions

Standing there, right between the mom who adopted me and the mom who gave birth to me, really made me think about how unusual my family situation was. The funeral was quiet, just soft music and the low murmur of people talking. But for me, it felt like a storm of emotions.

Looking at my adopted mom's face, filled with kindness and sadness, I saw just how complicated love and loss could be. She brought me into her family, cared for me, and now, she was right here with me as I dealt with something really personal. This moment made me realize how deep and strong the bond was between us.

CHAPTER 4.
LOSING AND REBUILDING LIFE

"Out of difficulties grow miracles." — *Jean de La Bruyère*

Living a stable life with fair health and a steady job, I managed my days like most people. But then everything started to shift. I never imagined life just doesn't surprise you. Sometimes, it slaps them!

It began subtly, with increasing tasks at work causing me enough discomfort to visit the doctor. Pain injections, physical therapy, light duty assignments, and the use of FMLA became part of my routine. Unbeknownst to me, these were the early signs of a major upheaval in my career and life.

Despite my efforts and the medical documentation I provided, my job chose to disregard my condition, labeling me AWOL instead of recognizing my medical needs. This led me to file a complaint with the EEOC for discrimination, particularly for denying me light duty. Little did I know, this would set off a chain of events leading to my removal from work and eventually becoming homeless.

In my desperation, I turned to every resource available. I sought help from the union, reached out to the late Senator Levin's office, and filed an EEOC complaint. Despite attending numerous arbitration meetings and fighting tirelessly for my rights, it all seemed futile. Now, it's April

16

2024, and there is still no settlement in sight. Yet, despite how delusional it may sound, I continue to place my trust in God for a positive outcome, believing that somehow, everything I lost will be restored.

During the early stages of filing my EEOC complaint, God placed something profound in my spirit: "God's timing supersedes my anxiety, weariness, and confusion." This reminder became my anchor, grounding me amidst the storm of uncertainty. Although I couldn't fathom it at the time, God was preparing me for something greater. The song "God is Preparing Me" resonated deeply within my heart, yet its full meaning remained a mystery.

So, I continue to wait, not passively, but with an active, steadfast faith. I trust that in God's perfect timing, everything will come to fruition. The trials I face today are merely stepping stones to a greater purpose He has in store for me. Through it all, I hold onto the belief that God's plans are always for my good, and He will restore what was lost in ways more profound than I could ever imagine.

Indeed, during this tumultuous period of homelessness, seven different families opened their homes to me. It was a critical juncture in my life, marked by the first eviction notice I ever received. Staring out of the picture window and looking up to the heavens, I declared, "Lord, over my dead body will I allow my nice furniture and belongings to be thrown out to the curb." At that moment, I had no plan for my furniture.

I remember sitting at the unemployment office, feeling utterly lost. Next to me was a woman in tears. My heart went out to her, and I gently asked, "Are you okay?" She looked up, her eyes red from crying, and shared, "My son and I lost everything in a house fire."

I paused, feeling a strange sense of providence at that moment. Here was someone who needed what I could no longer keep. "I have furniture," I said softly, not fully believing the words myself. "You can have it if you can arrange to pick it up."

Her face lit up with a mixture of surprise and relief. "Really? You would do that for us?"

I nodded, feeling the weight of my own burdens lighten ever so slightly. "Yes. It seems like it's meant to be."

As she thanked me, I felt a deep sense of peace and purpose. In the midst of my own struggles, I had found a way to help someone else. This simple act of kindness was a reminder that even in the darkest times, we can be a light to others.

When the woman arrived to collect the furniture, she was overwhelmed with gratitude, especially when I also gave her the picture that hung on the wall. Her joy was clear, expressing immense appreciation for both the living room and dinette set, and even more so for the picture. I felt there was no need to keep that beautiful picture when it could bring joy to someone else in such dire need.

"This picture," she said, tears welling up in her eyes, "it's exactly what we needed. Thank you... thank you so much."

Watching her happiness, I saw this as a clear sign that God had answered my prayers—nothing ended up discarded on my front lawn, and no sheriff was involved. This sequence of events marked the beginning of my recovery, starting with an invitation to stay at the first home that opened its doors to me.

As I settled into my first home, the kindness of the family enveloped me like a warm blanket. Each day was a step towards rebuilding my life. They didn't just provide a roof over my head; they offered companionship, understanding, and a sense of normalcy.

One evening, as I sat on the porch with the family, I found myself sharing my journey. "You know," I said, looking out at the setting sun, "I never expected any of this. But your kindness has given me hope."

The mother of the house smiled gently. "We're just glad we could help. Everyone needs a little support sometimes."

This experience taught me that miracles often arise from difficulties. Even when life seemed to be falling apart, there were moments of grace and unexpected connections that brought new hope. Through every trial, God was not only preparing me but also using me to make a difference in the lives of others.

The days that followed were filled with uncertainty and frequent relocations. Each of the seven families who took me in offered a temporary respite, a brief moment of stability in the chaos. Their kindness was a testament to the goodness that still exists in the world...

But some days were harder than others. One evening, as I lay on a borrowed bed, I wondered how much longer I could keep this up. The constant moving, the uncertainty... it was wearing me down. Yet, in those quiet moments, I would remind myself of the promise I felt deep within my heart. "God's timing," I whispered to myself, "God's timing will make sense of all this."

One morning, while sipping a cup of coffee at a friend's kitchen table, I found myself talking to God. "Why me, Lord? What am I supposed to learn from all this?" The answer didn't come immediately, but over time, I began to see the lessons in the trials. Patience, resilience, compassion... these were the gifts wrapped in the hardship.

In the end, it wasn't just about surviving the ordeal. It was about growing through it. Every challenge, every tear, every sleepless night was shaping me into a stronger, more empathetic person. And while the road ahead was still uncertain, I knew I wasn't walking it alone.

So here I am, still trusting, still hoping, still believing. The journey is far from over, but with each step, I am reminded of the strength within me and the unwavering support of a loving God. And perhaps, just perhaps, the miracles I seek are already unfolding, one small act of kindness at a time.

CHAPTER 5.
TURNING STRUGGLES INTO
STRENGTHS

"Sometimes the path you're on is not the one you would have chosen, but it's leading you exactly where you need to be."

I remember the countless hours spent in front of my computer, eyes straining at the screen as I scrolled through endless job postings. Each click represented a small hope, but more often than not, it was quickly dashed. The journey to find a job after earning both my bachelor's and master's degrees while being homeless was exhausting. How many more rejections can I take? I thought, feeling the weight of each unanswered application.

Six months had passed since graduation, and just when I started to believe that perhaps my efforts were in vain, my phone rang. It was Team Mental Health. Finally, a chance. They wanted to know if I was available for an interview. Available? After five years of homelessness from 2005 to 2010, and only working a part-time, temporary job for a brief period, I was beyond ready—this was the opportunity I had been waiting for.

The day of the interview felt crucial. As I sat in the waiting room, nerves buzzed through me like electricity. I knew this was more than just an interview—it was a doorway to stability, a chance to finally put my education and life experiences to work. When they called me in, I was greeted by a panel of focused faces.

One of the interviewers asked, "Can you tell us why you are interested in working with our agency?" I paused for a moment, gathering my thoughts. I spoke about my passion for mental health, my desire to learn more, and my commitment to serving those diagnosed with mental health conditions. I needed them to understand that this wasn't just a job for me—it was a calling.

And then, something shifted. Destiny, it seemed, was finally on my side. I was hired. My new role was as a care coordinator, working with a diverse group of people aged 18 and older—vulnerable adults, families, individuals living with both physical and mental disabilities, those battling substance abuse, the NGRI (Not Guilty by Reason of Insanity) population, homelessness, and more. For five months, I threw myself into the work, assisting clients by connecting them to on-site and off-site community resources, monitoring charts, and helping them apply for Medicaid, among other services.

Then, one day, my supervisor approached me with a smile. "Congratulations, Therapist Patricia," he said. I looked at him, puzzled. Therapist? "I'm a care coordinator," I replied, confusion clear in my voice. But he just smiled wider and repeated, "Congratulations, Therapist Patricia. You've been promoted to clinical therapist."

My Master of Social Work degree was finally being acknowledged, along with my Limited License LLMSW credentials. I had made it.

Transferring from a care coordinator to a therapist brought new challenges and responsibilities. My role now involved working closely with individuals who had experienced deep and varied traumas—substance abuse, foster care, adoption, involvement in the criminal justice system, sexual abuse, homelessness, and more. Each story I encountered carried its own weight, and each person I met was fighting their own battle.

I clearly recall one client who came into my office, her posture stiff, and her eyes guarded. As we began to talk, I gently asked about her childhood. Her tears welled up almost immediately. She hesitated, struggling to find the words. Eventually, she admitted that she had grown up in foster care. It was a moment filled with emotion, and I felt the pull to connect with her on a personal level. Should I tell her? I wondered. Would it help?

After a pause, I decided to share a small piece of my own story. "I understand how difficult that can be," I said softly. "I grew up in seven different foster homes myself." She looked up at me, surprise and recognition in her eyes. In that instant, the walls she had built began to crumble. She opened up more, sharing details she had never shared before. It was a powerful reminder of the strength that comes from shared experiences.

As a therapist, my role went beyond just listening. I worked with my clients to create individualized treatment plans that outlined how they could cope and navigate through their challenges. For some, this meant attending therapy sessions three times a month; for others, it was learning practical skills to manage anxiety and stress. Each plan was as unique as the person it was designed for, tailored to meet their specific needs and circumstances.

One of the most rewarding parts of my job was working with the homeless population. I facilitated group sessions, creating a safe space where members could learn to interact and communicate effectively. It wasn't just about providing therapy; it was about teaching them to respect each other's voices, to listen without interrupting, and to share their stories without fear of judgment. In those groups, I saw people who had been silenced by society find their voice again.

Each day as a therapist brought new challenges and new rewards. The work was not easy, but it was fulfilling in a way that words can hardly capture. This is where I'm meant to be, I often told myself, feeling a deep sense of purpose with every client I helped, every story I heard, and every life I touched.

Within the six years of being a care coordinator and clinical therapist, I faced a challenge that tested my courage and strength. Despite my dedication and the success I found in helping others, I struggled to pass the required licensing exam. I took it several times, each attempt ending in disappointment. How can I help others get through their own challenges when I can't seem to overcome this one? I often asked myself, feeling the sting of embarrassment and failure.

It was a bitter pill to swallow, having to use the same coping skills I taught my clients when facing their own setbacks. I had to confront my feelings of disappointment head-on, reminding myself that failure is not the end, but rather a step in the process. Yet, as the months passed, the pressure mounted. Eventually, my LLMSW credentials expired, and I had to step down from my role as a therapist.

I transitioned into a new position as an intake specialist, preparing documents for clients to begin their treatment. It wasn't where I wanted to be, but I did my best to adapt. Maybe this is just a temporary detour, I thought, trying to stay positive. But then, organizational policy changes led to yet another shift—I was moved from intake specialist to support coordinator, now working with LLBSW credentials.

This constant back-and-forth felt like a rollercoaster of emotions. I was depressed, irritated, and aggravated by the realization that my professional growth had been stunted. My dreams of promotions and salary increases seemed out of reach. Is this where my career stalls? I wondered, feeling the weight of it all pressing down on me.

But then, I came across a quote by Robert Branson: "Do not be embarrassed by your failures, learn from them, and start again." Those words struck a chord deep within me. Maybe this isn't the end—just a new beginning, I thought, trying to shift my perspective.

And then, something unexpected happened—a brighter side to these job titles began to reveal itself. My agency collaborated with a school for the developmentally disabled, and as part of my new role, I was given the opportunity to assist the staff and parents there. I helped educate them on the importance of petitioning for guardianship for students, linking them to community services for respite care, and more.

While my career path had taken unexpected turns, it had also led me to new and meaningful opportunities. The work I did at the school felt important, and impactful—like I was making a real difference in these families' lives.

So, despite the setbacks and the frustrations, I began to see the value in my journey. Maybe I'm not where I thought I'd be, but I'm exactly where I need to be right now. My experiences, both the mountains and the valleys, have given me a wealth of knowledge and a unique perspective that will, in time, prove to be even more valuable.

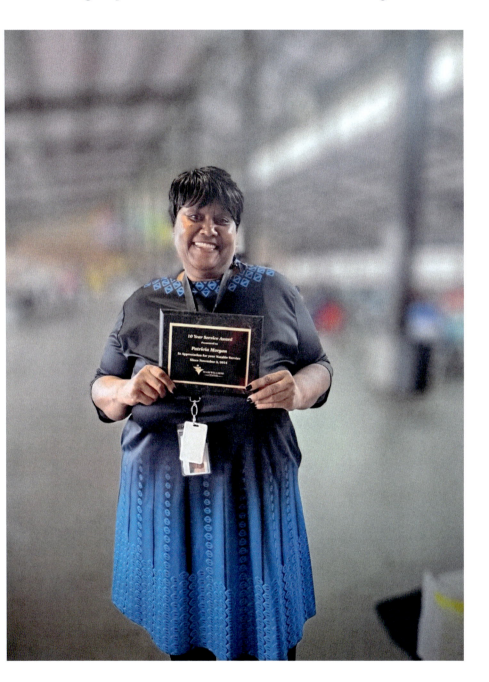

CHAPTER 6.
FROM HOMELESSNESS TO HOPE

"The struggles we endure today will be the 'good old days' we laugh about tomorrow." —Aaron Lauritsen

My personal experience with foster care, adoption, name changes, and homelessness has deeply shaped how I work in the human services field. Helping people deal with their anger, low self-esteem, and other mental stressors has become a central part of my work.

At one point, I wondered... since I was a foster child, would I one day become a foster parent? The thought stayed with me, hovering in the back of my mind. But the more I thought about it, the more I realized that the constant moving—from home to home, never knowing when I'd have to pack up and leave—isn't something I would want to put a child through. Especially a child already dealing with trust issues, attachment struggles, and anxiety.

Some might say, "Patricia, that's exactly why you should take in foster children." But... every time I thought about it, I remembered the feeling of uncertainty, of never knowing if the next home would be any better—or worse— than the last. How could I knowingly put a child through that same uncertainty?

It's not that I don't care... I care deeply. But I've walked that path, and I know how it feels to be a child in a system that often feels more like a maze than a refuge. I know the fear of the unknown, the anxiety of leaving behind what little stability you've managed to grasp, and the constant wondering if you'll ever truly belong anywhere.

Howbeit, I disagreed because if I struggled with that emotionally, it wouldn't be fair to subject an innocent child to my trauma. On the contrary, I can empathize with my clients and people in general without being judgmental. I understand their pain, their fears... their longing for stability. But I also know my own limits, and I've come to accept that my past experiences, while valuable in understanding others, would make it too difficult for me to take on the role of a foster parent.

I remember back in Undergrad, in one of my classes, a fellow student shared how stressful it was working with

Child Protective Services (CPS) and moving children from one home to another. It was then I knew... working for CPS or being a foster mother was not for me. It would be a constant trigger, a relentless reminder of my own past, and I would forever be wondering... when would the social worker come and take the child away?

On another note, I found that working with the homeless population significantly impacted my ability to connect with people on a deeper level. Helping someone secure employment, assisting them in finding low-income housing... these moments were transformative. They were more than just victories—they were steps toward restoring dignity and hope in lives that had been shattered by circumstances often beyond their control.

The days that followed receiving those keys were a mix of joy and uncertainty. I moved into my new space with a sense of relief, but also a lingering fear... What if this, too, was temporary? What if the stability I craved was just an illusion, ready to be snatched away at any moment?

Each of the seven families who took me in during those years of homelessness had offered me more than just a place to stay—they had given me a brief respite from the chaos that seemed to define my life. Their kindness was a reminder that even in the darkest times, there were still people willing to extend a hand, to share what little they had. But some days... some days were harder than others.

One evening, as I lay on a borrowed bed, the weight of it all pressed down on me. How much longer could I keep this up? The constant moving, the lack of a place to call my own... it was wearing me down, bit by bit. The physical exhaustion was one thing, but the emotional toll was something else entirely. I was tired—not just in my body, but in my spirit.

And yet, in those quiet, lonely moments, when it felt like the world had turned its back on me, there was a small voice inside, a whisper of hope that refused to be silenced. "God's timing..." I would remind myself, clinging to the belief that there was a purpose behind all this pain. "God's timing will make sense of all this."

It wasn't easy to hold onto that belief, especially when the days felt endless and the nights even longer. There were times when I questioned everything—my choices, my faith, my strength. But even in those moments of doubt, I knew that giving up was not an option. I had come too far, endured too much, to let despair take over.

So, I kept moving forward, one day at a time, one step at a time. There were small victories—moments of light in the darkness. Finding a job, securing a stable place to live, and reconnecting with parts of myself that had been lost along the way. Each of these milestones was a testament to the resilience I had discovered within myself—a resilience I hadn't known I possessed until life demanded it of me.

And as I moved through this journey, I began to see the bigger picture. The trials, the heartaches, the moments of desperation... they weren't just obstacles to overcome. They were shaping me, molding me into someone who could understand, on a deeply personal level, the struggles of those I was meant to help. God was not only preparing me but also using me to make a difference in the lives of others.

CHAPTER 7.
PIECING TOGETHER THE PAST

"The bond that links your true family is not one of blood, but of respect and joy in each other's life." — Richard Bach

People usually ask me, what was your relationship like with your various family members? And when asked which family, I ponder... Foster family? Adopted family? Biological family? Or the friends who've become like family? The definition of family extends beyond mere bloodlines, it encompasses ancestry, genealogy, and those deeply ingrained connections that define our existence.

Despite the unique bonds I've shared with all whom I've called family, there remained a void—a major disconnection from my biological mother. This disconnection often led me to daydream about what life might have been like under her care. Yes, I was aware of her struggles with schizophrenia from an early age, yet this knowledge did little to dampen my yearning for her maternal love... the kind of instinctive comfort that a baby feels in the womb, warmth, protection, and nurture.

In each foster home, my basic needs were met, food, clothes, shelter—but what I yearned for went beyond the physical. I longed for that inherent maternal bond, which, despite the best efforts of my caregivers, always felt just out of reach...

When I started reading about schizophrenia, everything began to make a little more sense. This illness made life so hard for my mom. It must have been really tough for her, every day. The more I understood, the more I realized why it might have been better for me to grow up away from her. It's a sad thought, but maybe it kept me from seeing some really hard times.

Finding out that mental illness wasn't just with my mom but ran in the family made things clearer too. It was like discovering a missing piece in a puzzle that had puzzled me for years. This wasn't just about my mother; the challenge of mental health was into the roots of our family tree. This knowledge shed light on why my grandmother raised my brother instead of me. I had always felt a sense of rejection, wondering why I was the one left out. It felt as though I had been picked last for a team in gym class, not because I couldn't play but because of fears I didn't understand.

As I grew older and understood more about schizophrenia and its impacts, I started to piece together the reasons behind my family's decisions. Maybe there were real concerns about my safety, fears that being closer to my mother's unpredictable condition could lead to situations too tough for a child to handle. It's like walking on a frozen pond; they were afraid the ice might crack under my feet.

These insights didn't heal all the pain, some scars are too deep for that, but they began to make sense of the chaos that shadowed my childhood. Recognizing this didn't take away the hurt completely, but it was like finding directions in a forest I'd been lost in for too long.

It's tough, trying to piece together these fragments from the past, like assembling a broken vase. Each piece fits somewhere, and understanding where helps it all make more sense. Knowing that these decisions weren't made lightly or randomly but out of a deep-seated concern for my wellbeing helps me grapple with the past. This journey of understanding doesn't erase the pain, but it lightens the load, a little at a time, offering a clearer path forward.

I started seeing things in a new light. Realizing how tough life was for my mom helped me understand why I had to grow up away from her. Life is hard for everyone in different ways, and this helped me let go of some of the hurt I felt about not having her around.

Before, I often felt bitter and wondered why things had to be the way they were. But as I began to understand her struggles better, I saw that she had her own battles. She wasn't just dealing with life; she was fighting hard against her own mind every day. This didn't make everything okay, but it helped me feel a bit more peace about our situation.

And well, this is life, maybe... complicated, yet it keeps going. It's like a river that doesn't stop flowing, even when it hits rocks or falls over cliffs. Every twist and turn, every rapid and quiet pool, tells a part of my story. Learning about my family's struggles with mental health, understanding why decisions were made the way they were, it's all part of get through this river.

And the truth is, you never really know how tough you are until being tough becomes the only option you have. Life has a way of pushing you to your limits, testing you in ways you never expected. It's in those moments, when all other choices seem to fade away, that when you get to learn and understand things about life. And, that's what….I learned the hard

CHAPTER 8.
THROUGH THE STORM, WE STAND

"Faith isn't about seeing the finish line; it's about trusting the journey, even when the path is uncertain and the road is long."

People often ask me how I've managed to keep my faith through everything... the homelessness, the legal battles, the constant upheaval. Sometimes, even I wonder how I've held on. There were so many voices telling me to let it go, to accept that what happened at the Post Office was just one of those things you have to move past.

"Patricia, you'll never win against the government. Just move on with your life," they'd say. And believe me, I tried. I pushed forward, working on my degrees, finding jobs, securing a place to live. I thought I had put it all behind me... but some things just don't leave you.

The world has changed so much since then. There's been war and unrest, a pandemic that upended everything, new presidents, and shifts in society that none of us could have imagined. I've lost family members, dear friends, and yet... the class action lawsuit, with thousands of people like me, is still unresolved. It's almost surreal, living through so many personal changes while that fight remains ongoing, like a stubborn shadow that just won't fade away.

There were times I looked at myself and thought, Am I being foolish? Holding onto something I should have let go of a long time ago? I'd ask myself if I was misinterpreting faith... twisting it into something stubborn instead of something hopeful. But every time those doubts crept in, I'd feel something shift—like a whisper inside telling me to keep believing, to keep pushing forward.

I remember one night, sitting alone with my Bible, feeling completely overwhelmed. I flipped it open, almost at random, and landed on Isaiah 55:8: "For my thoughts are not your thoughts, nor are your ways My ways, says the Lord." It hit me so hard that I had to stop and catch my breath. It was as if God was saying, "Trust me, even when you can't see the plan."

And then there was Job 5:12: "He frustrates the devices of the crafty, so that their hands cannot carry out their plans." In 2004 I read this and I've clung to it ever since. It's been a constant reminder that no matter how powerful the opposition seems, there's a higher power at work, making sure that justice will eventually prevail.

When I felt like I didn't have the strength to keep going, I turned to 2 Samuel 22:40: "For you have armed me with strength for the battle." Those words became my mantra. I'd repeat them over and over, letting them sink into my spirit, reminding myself that I was not alone in this fight. That every trial, every setback, was making me stronger, preparing me for something I couldn't yet understand.

I know it sounds strange, but my faith grew stronger in those moments of doubt and fear. It was like every time I questioned if I should let go, I'd find myself drawn closer to

God's promises. I could feel Him nudging me, saying, "Not yet. Keep going."

Psalm 59:9 became especially important to me: "I will wait for You, O You his Strength; for God is my defense." And verse 10: "My God of mercy shall come to meet me; God shall let me see my desire on my enemies." Those verses spoke directly to my heart. They were a promise that, no matter how long it took, God was watching, God was listening, and God would act. It was a hard truth to hold onto because waiting isn't easy, especially when you've been waiting for years.

But wait, I did. I had to. Not because I didn't have a choice, but because I believed—truly believed—that this journey was about more than just me. I wasn't just fighting for my own justice; I was fighting for everyone who's ever been wronged, for everyone who's ever felt powerless against a system that seemed too big to fight.

There were days when I thought about what it would feel like to let it all go... to stop pushing, to walk away from the fight. Maybe I'd feel lighter, maybe the weight of all this anger and frustration would finally lift. But every time I thought about quitting, I'd remember why I started in the first place. This wasn't just about a job. It was about standing up for what was right. It was about my dignity, my self-respect, and yes, my faith.

I know that faith isn't about getting everything you want. It's not about a life free from struggle or pain. It's about trusting in something bigger than yourself, even when everything around you is falling apart. It's about believing that, somehow, all the pieces will come together for good, even when you can't see how.

So, I kept going. Day by day, I got up, I prayed, I fought. And in those quiet moments, when it felt like the world was too heavy to carry, I'd close my eyes and remind myself of all the times God had been faithful before. I'd think about the nights I cried myself to sleep, not knowing where I'd find the strength to keep going, and yet... somehow, I always did.

I don't know how this story will end. Maybe the Classaction will be resolved, maybe it won't. But I do know this: I've already won something far more important. I've won the battle for my soul, for my faith, for my belief in justice and truth. And that... that is something no one can ever take away from me.

Because faith isn't about getting what you want. It's about believing in what you can't see. It's about holding on when everyone else tells you to let go. It's about standing firm, not because you're stubborn, but because you know in your heart that you're standing on something solid. Something true.

And so, I wait... not just for justice, but for whatever God has in store. Because I know that His plans are better than mine, His ways higher than my ways. And that's enough. For now, that's enough.

CHAPTER 9.
SHAPED BY SHADOWS, GUIDED BY LIGHT

Out of difficulties grow miracles." — *Jean de La Bruyère*

Life has a way of teaching us lessons through our deepest pains and greatest challenges. Looking back, one of the hardest lessons I've learned is that I've been grieving the loss of my identity since childhood. It started with not being raised by my biological mother, never knowing my biological father, and feeling the weight of secrets kept from me by my biological family. My grandmother chose to raise my brother instead of me, and that left a void I've carried for years.

But these losses… they've shaped me into a more empathetic person. I've learned to care deeply for others who are going through hard times because I know what it feels like to struggle. I used to think homelessness meant seeing someone on the street holding a sign for food or money, but now I know… there are so many versions of homelessness. I remember watching Judge Mathis one day when he told a man, "Well, you're homeless—you don't have an address." That hit me hard, and I thought, "Oh wow, I'm homeless too."

That realization changed me. It taught me not to judge, to listen more carefully to people's stories, and to give back.

Whether it's donating to homeless charities or making care packages with socks and toiletries… I've learned to help in ways I never imagined before.

Spiritually, emotionally, I've also grown. Through therapy, prayer, and spiritual guidance, I've learned to forgive—not just for others but for my own healing. There was a time when I wished harm on those who hurt me, especially my foster father and other men who abused me. But over time, I realized that holding onto that pain was only hurting me. I talked about my hurt in therapy, prayed about it, and chose to stop dwelling on it… I didn't forget it, but I learned to let go of the bitterness that kept me trapped.

I also understand how hard it is for foster and adopted children to fit in with a family. We try so hard to be accepted for who we are, but often, we feel misunderstood. When I expressed my feelings as a child, it wasn't anger I was showing—it was hurt. But that hurt often gets mistaken for something else, and we're left feeling like no one really sees us.

These experiences have shaped who I am today. They've taught me to be more understanding, more compassionate, and most of all… to listen with an open heart. Through every hardship, I've learned that life's greatest lessons often come from its most difficult moments.

Made in the USA
Middletown, DE
06 February 2025

70963042R10031